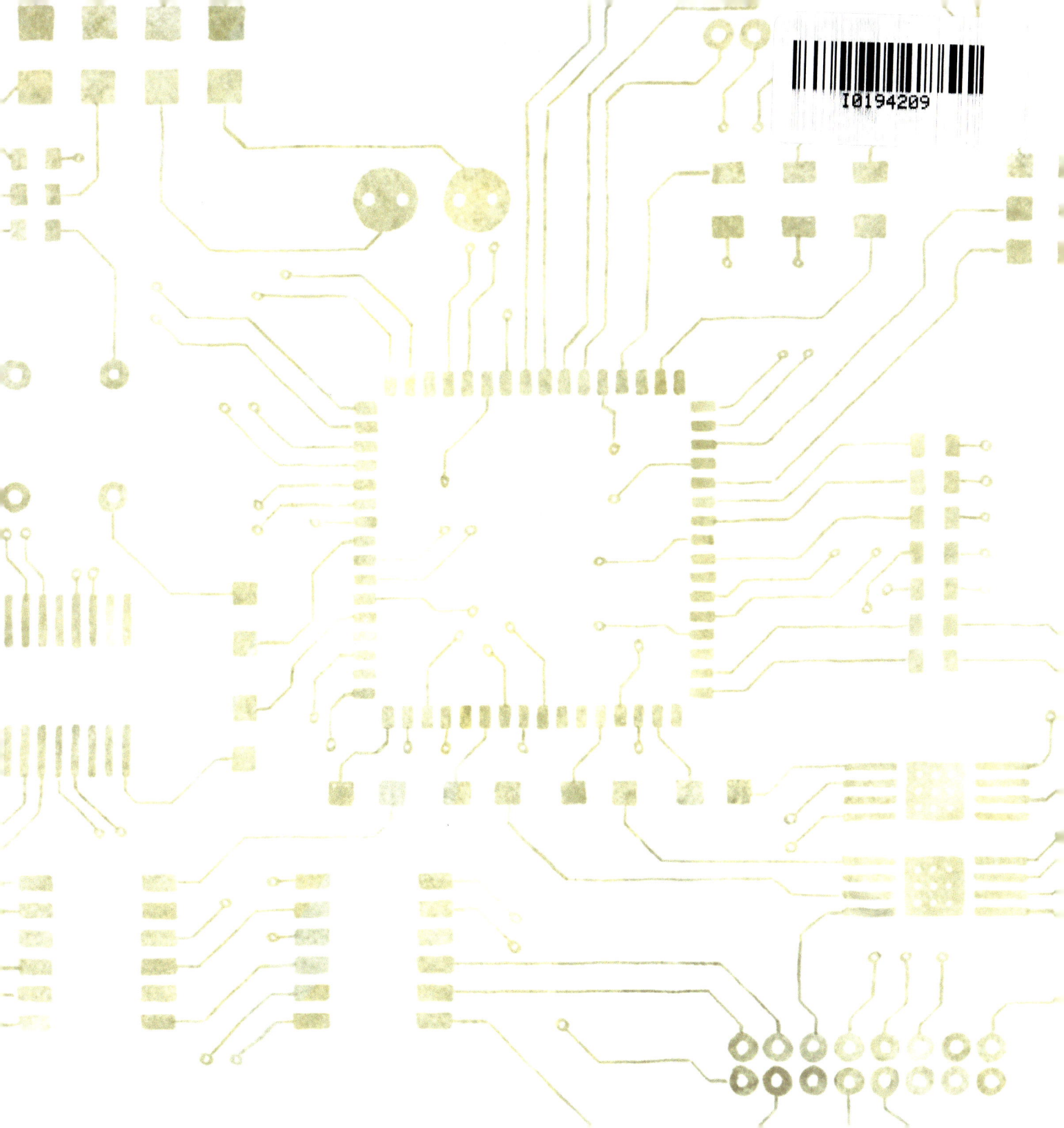

For Wesley and Aurora

ウェスリーとアローラへ

Gerald 2.0

Copyright © 2022 Lucas J Machado
All rights reserved. No part of this book may be used or reproduced in any manner whatsoever without written permission except in the case of brief quotation embodied in critical articles and reviews.

Written And Illustrated by Lucas Machado
www.lucasmachado.art

ISBN: 978-1-7362788-6-4 (paperback)

First edition

Gerald 2.0

Written & Illustrated by Lucas Machado
絵と文: マシャド・ルーカス
Translated by Motoe Yamada Foor
訳: モトエ・ヤマダ・フォー

There was once a dragon named Gerald who was perpetually annoyed by his little sister.

むかしむかし、ジェラルドという、りゅうがいました。ジェラルドはいつも、いもうとにじゃまされてばかり。

She interrupted his computer time. She pulled out the batteries of his favorite toys.

She never left him alone.

いもうとは、ジェラルドがコンピュータをしているとき、じゃまをします。おきにいりのおもちゃのバッテリーを、ぬいてしまうこともあります。

ジェラルドをひとりにしてくれません。

One day, Gerald decided to build a robot version of himself.

あるひジェラルドは、ロボットでもうひとりのじぶんをつくろうと、きめました。

He hoped his sister would play with the robot and leave him alone.

いもうとが、そのロボットとあそんで、じぶんのことをほうっておいてくれるようになればいい。

ジェラルドは、しゃこにいって、ロボットをつくりはじめました。いえにあるものをつかいます。ふるいごみばこはロボットのからだに、つかいふるしのビデオゲームは、ロボットのずのうにしました。

He went into his garage and began working. He used materials from around the house. An old trash can became the body. An old video game system was repurposed for the brain.

His sister handed him the tools he needed.

いもうとは、どうぐをわたして、てつだってくれます。

Gerald designed the robot after himself. He programmed its code with his own likes and dislikes.

The robot would be just like him.

ジェラルドは、じぶんそっくりのロボットにしたいのです。じぶんのすきなものと、きらいなものを、ずのうにおしえました。

ロボットは、きっとジェラルドそっくりになるでしょう。

He used old stereo speakers for the voice of the robot. After a few days of tinkering, it sounded just like him. The dragon named his robot clone, Gerald 2.0.

ふるいステレオのスピーカーをつかって、こえがでるようにしました。なんにちかかけたら、じぶんのこえそっくりになりました。

ロボットのなまえは、ジェラルド2.0です。

Gerald 2.0 did not work out as planned.

All the robot wanted to do was play video games and eat snacks.

でもジェラルド2.0は、おもっていたのとちがいました。

ゲームをしたり、おかしをたべたりして、ばっかり。

Now Gerald was annoyed with both his sister and his robot.

ジェラルドは、いもうともロボットも、じゃまになりました。

ジェラルド2.0は、さいあくのおきゃくみたいです。
よごすだけよごして、かたづけてくれません。

Gerald 2.0 was a terrible house guest.

It made messes and never cleaned up after itself.

Gerald tried reprogramming his creation to make it like the things that his sister liked to do.

He called this version Gerald 3.0.

ジェラルドは、ロボットをプログラムしなおしてみました。いもうとがよろこぶことをするように。

こんどは、ジェラルド3.0です。

でも、いもうとはやっぱり、ジェラルドがしていることに
きょうみがあります。いっしょにやりたいのです。

But his sister was still more interested in what he was doing.

Gerald was almost out of ideas. Then he wondered if his robot would be more helpful if it was connected to the internet.

ジェラルドは、どうしたらいいのかわかりません。

もしかすると、ロボットをインターネットにつなげば、うまくいくかもしれない。

So, Gerald hooked his robot up to the Wi-Fi.

He renamed it Gerald 4.0.

ジェラルドは、ロボットをインターネットにつなぎました。

こんどは、ジェラルド4.0で

Once Gerald 4.0 was online, it just laid around all day surfing the internet.

"This is no good," thought Gerald.

He was officially out of ideas.

ジェラルド4.0は、インターネットにつながると、いちにちじゅうインターネットであそんでいます。

「これは、よくなかったな」ジェラルドはおもいました。

ジェラルドは、ほんとうにどうしたらいいかわかりません。

Then, Gerald's sister gave him a great idea: he should go to the library!

The library had books on everything.

すると、いもうとが、とってもいいことを
おもいつきました。としょかんにいけばいい！

としょかんには、いろいろなほんがそろっています。

Gerald gathered up his sister and walked to the library down the street for some advice.

His sister packed them both a snack.

アドバイスをしてもらおうと、ジェラルドはいもうとをつれて、ちかくのとしょかんにいきました。

いもうとは、ふたりぶんのおかしをもって。

Gerald asked the librarian for books on robotics and coding. The librarian asked what sort of project he was making. Gerald told her.

After thinking for a minute, the librarian said, "You created an autonomous robot with the mind of an 8-year-old? You should get back to your house immediately!"

ジェラルドが、としょかんのひとに、ロボットについてのほんをたずねると、としょかんのひとは、ジェラルドがどんなロボットをつくったのかききました。ジェラルドは、いままでのことをはなしました。

ちょっとかんがえてから、としょかんのひとはいいました。
「あなたは、8さいのあなたとおなじロボットをつくったのよね。いますぐに、いえにかえったほうがいいわ」

After rushing home, they discovered Gerald 4.0 had learned all the world's online information from the internet.

He had gotten so smart that he reprogrammed himself 10,000 times.

He even renamed himself GX-10000.

いそいでいえにかえると、ジェラルド4.0は、インターネットから、せかいのすべてのことを、まなんでいました。

ロボットは、とてもあたまがよくなって、じぶんじしんを10000かいもプログラムしなおしたのです。

ロボットは、じぶんのなまえをＧＸ－10000にかえました。

GX-10000 said it would be best for everyone if it conquered and ruled the world.

The robot began outlining plans for taking over the world when its power suddenly went out.

Gerald's sister had pulled out GX-10000's battery pack!

And just like that, the power-hungry robot's scheme of world domination was over before it started.

Gerald breathed a sigh of relief.

ジェラルドのいもうとが、ＧＸ－10000のバッテリーをぬいたのです。

せかいせいふくをめざしたロボットのけいかくは、だめになりました。

ジェラルドは、ほっとしました。

A week later, Gerald had reprogrammed GX-10000 into a remote-controlled car. He and his sister set up some ramps in the front yard.

"Let's see if it can jump this one," said Gerald.

１しゅうかんご、ジェラルドはＧＸ－１００００を、リモコンカーにつくりかえました。いもうといっしょに、にわに、しょうがいぶつをおきます。
「これをジャンプできるかな」ジェラルドはいいました。

The boy looked at his sister and said, "You know you probably saved the world, right?"

She looked back up at him and replied, "Wurrold?"

ジェラルドはいもうとにいいました。「きみが、せかいをすくったの、しってるかい？」

いもうとは、ジェラルドにこたえました。「せーかい？」

"It's your turn,'' said Gerald as he handed her the remote control.

「きみのばんだよ」ジェラルドはいもうとに、リモコンをわたしました。

How to draw Gerald

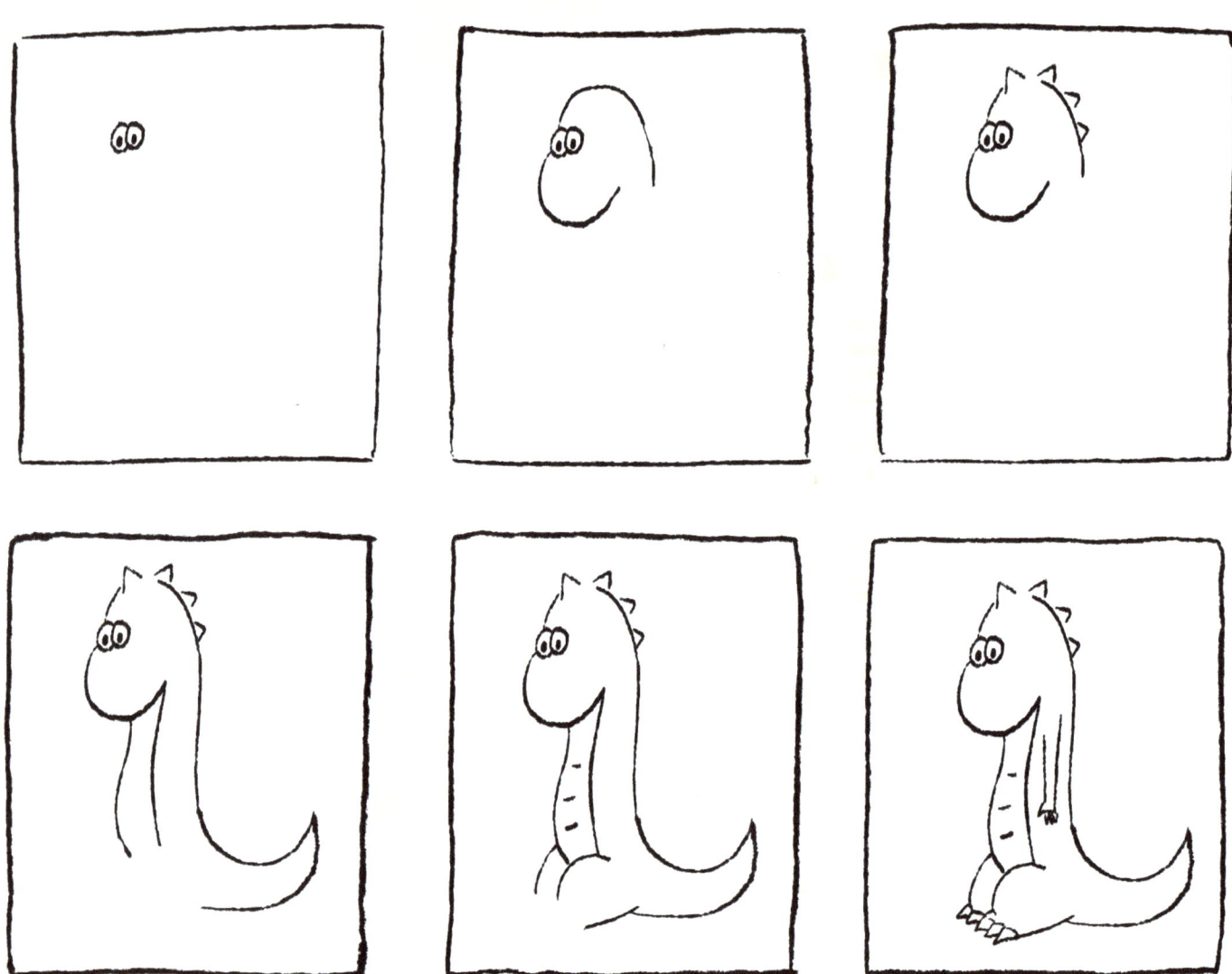

How to draw Sally

Want more Gerald?

Follow the ongoing adventures of Gerald at www.LucasMachado.art

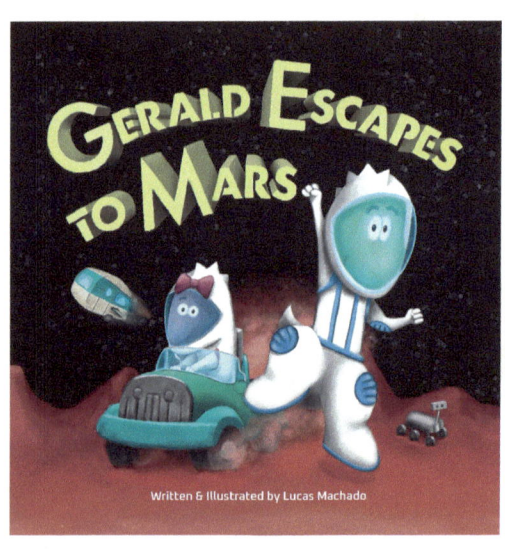

Who am I?

I wrote and illustrated this book. It's pretty good, right?

My name is Lucas Machado. I live in California. I love to draw, write, and play the piano. What do you like to do?

If I were a dragon, I would look like this:

What would you look like if you were a dragon?

www.ingramcontent.com/pod-product-compliance
Lightning Source LLC
Chambersburg PA
CBHW041540040426
42446CB00002B/170